DANCING IN THE MOON

HARCOURT BRACE JOVANOVICH, PUBLISHERS
SAN DIEGO   NEW YORK   LONDON

DANCING IN THE MOON

Fritz Eichenberg

COUNTING RHYMES

BY *Fritz Eichenberg*

To Albert Einstein
who liked
children, animals and numbers

Printed in the United States of America

ISBN 0-15-221443-7

M N O P

1 raccoon dancing in the moon

2 moose scaring a papoose

3 jaguars playing guitars

4 pandas resting on verandas

5 dragons pulling wagons

6 kangaroos selling news

7 baboons drawing cartoons

8 llamas wearing pajamas

9 bears saying their prayers

10 cats trying on hats

11 geese disturbing the peace

12 pets playing quartets

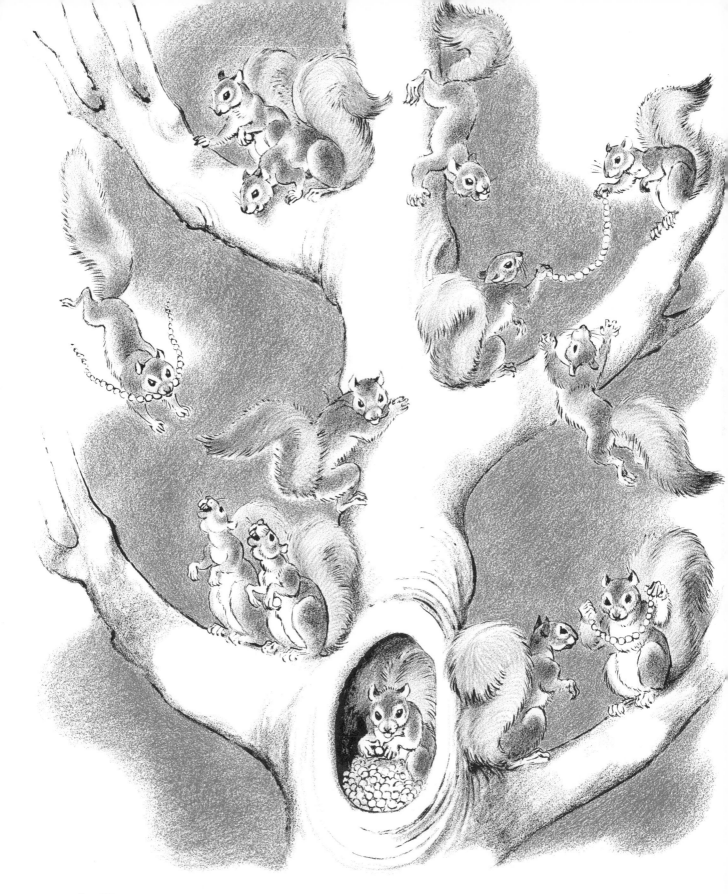

13 squirrels collecting pearls

14 mice skating on ice

15 hounds making sounds

16 pigs dancing jigs

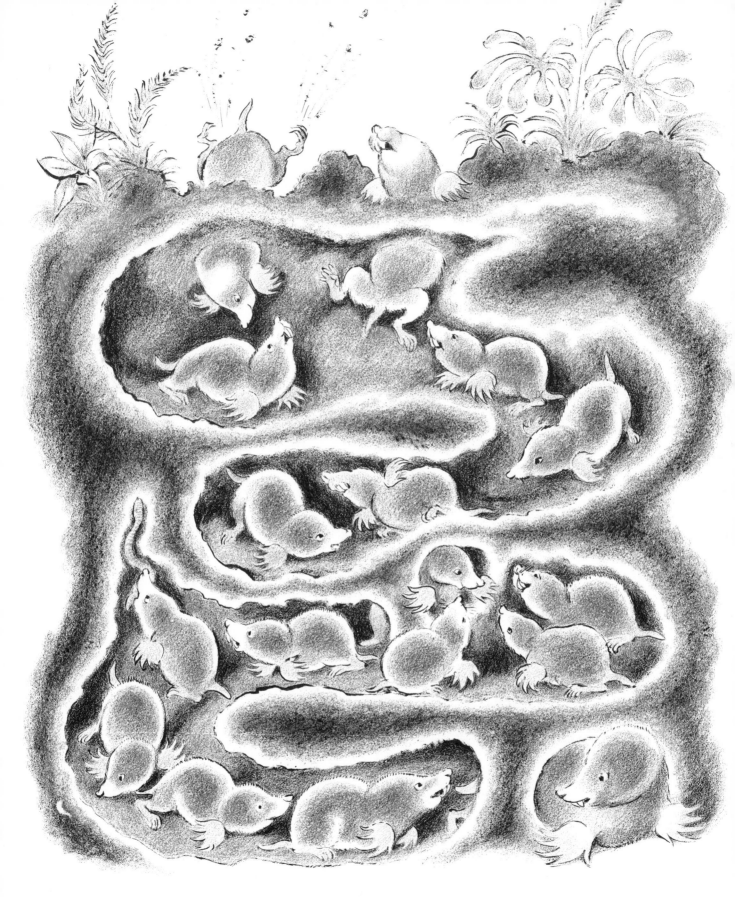

17 moles digging holes

18 frogs sitting on logs

19 seals enjoying their meals

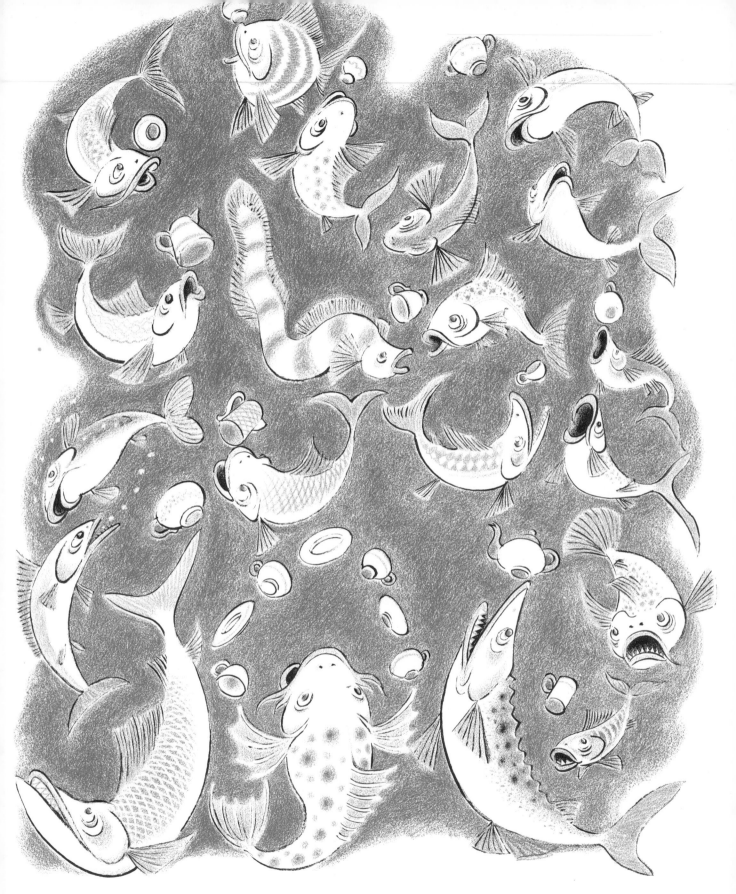

20 fishes juggling dishes